A Thread of Hope

Dennis Jernigan

innovo PUBLISHING

Published by
Innovo Publishing LLC
www.innovopublishing.com
1-888-546-2111

Providing Full-Service Publishing Services for
Christian Authors, Artists, and Organizations: Hardbacks, Paperbacks,
eBooks, Audiobooks, Music, and Film

A THREAD OF HOPE

ISBN 13: 978-1-61314-287-5

Cover Design & Interior Layout by Innovo Publishing LLC
Illustrations by Kim Merritt

Printed in the United States of America
U.S. Printing History
First Edition: August 2015

A Thread of Hope

Dennis Jernigan

A specially priced read-along version of this story narrated by Dennis Jernigan,
including an original song written and performed by Dennis Jernigan,
is available in the Audiobooks section of the eStore at innovopublishing.com.

Somewhere in the darkness a little girl sat alone—
although she wasn't really a little girl anymore.
Still, she felt like one. Pain had given way to
numbness a long time ago. Every once in a while,
a glimmer of emotion tried to make its way into
the open, but she'd grown too wise to allow those
little glimmers to see the light of day. Numbness
was better than pain—or so she thought. She'd
grown up in such a different world than the eye is
accustomed to seeing. What had been normal for
her and her family would be considered perverse
by anyone else—that is, if they could see behind
her veil of secrecy.

Her life hadn't started out this way. Her earliest memories include a dress her momma had given her—a twirl-around dress, she called it, because she could spin around in an impromptu pirouette and watch as the skirt lifted in flight to her dance of joy. Her good memories also included a little doll that her grandmother had made and presented to her on her fifth birthday.

The doll had rosy red cheeks and beautiful, long auburn hair, with eyes that would open and close. She wore a simple dress, slippers, and a plain white apron. What drew one's attention to the doll's apron was the single golden thread that weaved its way through the material like a gently meandering stream, adding just the right amount of glitter to a rather inconspicuous little toy.

Her grandmother told her to remember, whenever she felt a little sad or lonely, that the doll was given to her by someone who loved her very much. She told her the golden thread that ran through the doll's apron was a symbol of hope, and in the same way that thread ran its simple course through the cloth, hope would always be there running through the fabric of her life. A rather weighty concept for such a little girl, but she had never forgotten her grandmother's words. To help seal this in the little girl's heart, her grandmother taught her this song:

Did you know that someone loves you—
Loves you lavishly?
Loves you more than the whole wide world!
That someone is me.

When you fall, I'll pick up the pieces.
When you hurt, I'll bind up your wound.
When you're alone or afraid,
I'll be right where you are,
And I love you.

Yet here she was, so many years later—alone, abandoned, afraid. Worn out and weary from simply trying to survive.

And packed somewhere in the one frayed bag that held all her worldly belongings was the little doll she had come to call Hope. At times the girl had wanted to crush the doll, or burn it, or just get it away from her, but for some reason she had never been able to let go. By now the doll's dress had become frayed, and the golden thread had faded to dull brown. The girl remembered her grandmother's words—that hope would be there running through the fabric of her life. Humph! The series of events she called her "life" could in no way be considered hopeful.

Having had hope crushed so many times and been rejected and abandoned by so many people, the girl changed the words to her grandmother's song:

Is anybody out there?
Can anybody see that who I am on the outside
is really not me?

When I fall, who will pick up the pieces?
When I hurt, who will bind up my wound?
When I'm alone or afraid, will anybody be there?
I'd like to know who…

Reaching the underside of a bridge on a lonely stretch of road, she threw her bag to the ground and sat there. Nowhere to go. No one to talk to. As far as she knew, there was no one who even knew or cared that she existed. If she could start a fire, maybe the glow of the flame would lift her spirit and at least warm her body. Groping through her bag for a lighter, her hand brushed against the little doll, Hope. Sad to say, but a little tinge of emotion electrified her heart in that one brief touch. Even sadder to think that an inanimate object had become her best friend.

Finding enough dry wood and kindling nestled beneath the dry underbelly of that old bridge, she was able to start a small fire. And she was right; it did make her feel better. Warm.

She picked up the doll and began to retrace the memories invoked by every frayed edge. Around the doll's arms and legs were threads of memories she had collected through the years. There was a thread for the time her father had beaten her for interrupting his TV time and had locked her away in the closet for three days. She had unraveled a thread from the carpet and decorated Hope just to pass the time—just to keep her sanity.

Then there was the thread representing the countless verbal assaults and insults she had suffered from her mother, who always seemed to be jealous of her own daughter. She never quite understood the reasons why her mother felt the need to put her down, especially in front of her dad.

Her parents had always gone out of their way to have the finest things, biggest homes, designer clothes, and whatever else seemed to make them feel as if they were the pride of the neighborhood. Even as a girl, she knew this surely wasn't the way a normal family ought to live, but it had come to be her normal—pretty and polite and well-received in public, but hiding a world of pain, sorrow, and suffering that none of her friends would have believed.

Yes, Hope had come to have quite an array of threads wrapped around her arms and legs, each one representing a painful memory of suffering and sorrow.

As she journeyed back to her painful past, here were two white strands of thread wrapped snugly around the waist of the little doll. She had tried to forget these for so many reasons. The first thread represented the night when she was twelve years old and had given birth to a precious little girl. She had not even gotten to hold the baby but had managed to pull at the white cotton edges of the blanket as the infant was pulled from her trembling arms. The plain white thread reminded her of the helplessness she had felt when the man came into her room so many times. Her own relative. She had told her mother, but her mother only told her to watch her tongue.

The second thread represented the little boy who had been taken from her when she was fourteen. Again, she had managed to grasp one little thread as he was taken away. This strand reminded her of how odd she had felt when her own family pretended nothing had happened, yet at the same time seemed to silently blame her for the predicament she had placed them all in—as if she had somehow had a choice in the matter! Even when she had tried to go to the authorities in her small town, she was told to stop talking nonsense.

The threads of her life were wrapped around a little doll named Hope, but hope wasn't even remotely possible.

Is anybody out there?
Can anybody see that who I am on the outside
is really not me?

When I fall, who will pick up the pieces?
When I hurt, who will bind up my wound?
When I'm alone or afraid, will anybody be there?
I'd like to know who…

Having been warmed by the fire, the girl was able to rest. As she thought about her life, her eyes grew tired, and she drifted off to sleep. Dreams had never been sweet in her life, but tonight the torment of the nightmares she had grown accustomed to was simply not there. Instead, she found herself twirling 'round and 'round in her twirl-around dress, dancing for her grandmother again. So free, so full of joy. She danced and danced for hours as her grandmother sang the old lullaby:

Did you know that someone loves you—
Loves you lavishly?
Loves you more than the whole wide world!
That someone is me.

When you fall, I'll pick up the pieces.
When you hurt, I'll bind up your wound.
When you're alone or afraid, I'll be right where you are,
And I love you.

As the song faded, her dream continued. Only now it wasn't her grandmother who was in the dream, but a man. A shepherd!? Sheep were contentedly grazing in the meadow around him, and he was beckoning the girl to follow Him—so she did. As they went from lush pastures and deep, flowing streams to wonderful mountain vistas, her heart felt like it would leap right out of her chest at the sheer freedom and acceptance she felt in his presence.

Then the journey took them to a place of terrible and unmentionable horror. He led her down through the darkest of valleys, full of sinister, glowing eyes peering out from the crevices of every gully through which they passed. Instead of the serenity of calm meadows, now the darkness was pierced with shrieks and groans of fear and pain.

He pulled her closer to his side. She sensed danger in her surroundings, yet she felt safe next to him. It was obvious that everyone around her was there to torment her and to take her life, but the shepherd never allowed the enemy to touch her.

To her amazement, he led her to the most extravagant feast she had ever seen. Right there in the midst of her enemies, the shepherd had prepared an elaborate smorgasbord! Taking a seat, they dined for what seemed like an eternity. The shepherd then picked up the girl and carried her to a secluded forest glen where the shrieking had been replaced with absolute quiet and the darkness, with the brightness of a full moon. She remembered men of her childhood who had carried her away in fear, but she felt none of that in this moment. Lying in peace on his shoulder, she was soothed to sleep even in her dream by the shepherd's simple song:

*When everything you are just seems to fall apart, and you're
alone in the dark,
Sorrow, like endless rain, no longer hides the pain.
And now you've drifted too far.
Come down from the ledge of your own broken heart.
Run here to my open arms where you can fall apart.*

*I'll be your light in dark. I'll be right where you are.
I'll hold you close through the pain.
I'll calm the raging tide. I'll be right by your side.
I'll shelter you from the rain.
Put your head on my shoulder.
Put your head on my shoulder and rest.*

*No more tears left to cry—wishing that you could die
and make this hurt go away!
This endless raging storm has left your heart so torn,
You simply can't see a way.
Come down from the ledge of your own broken heart.
Run here to my open arms where you can fall apart!*

*I'll be your light in dark. I'll be right where you are.
I'll hold you close through the pain.
I'll calm the raging tide. I'll be right by your side.
I'll shelter you from the rain.
Put your head on my shoulder.
Put your head on my shoulder and rest.*

The song ended, and the girl opened her eyes to find that the shepherd had carried her back to the bridge where the dream had first begun. She was so full of questions, and she sensed that her dream would end soon.

"Who are you?" she asked.

"My name is Jesus, and I've been watching over you for a long time."

"So why did You allow all these terrible things to ruin my life?"

"I allowed them, yes, but your life is far from ruined. Like your little doll, Hope, I've been with you every step of the way. And like the golden thread that runs through her apron, I've been here through every one of your sorrows, constantly calling for you to come to Me. If you never knew the dryness of the desert, would you ever know the sweetness of the rain when it falls? If you never knew the sorrow and pain of life, would you ever be able to fully experience the comfort and healing I now offer you? Like those extra threads you've added to Hope through the course of your journey, your life may seem frayed and frazzled and beyond hope, but here's what I'll do if you'll let me."

And the Shepherd took the doll from the girl and began unraveling all the threads that had come to represent pain and sorrow and suffering. And right then and there, He began weaving a beautiful tapestry. What had just a few moments earlier been a shambled mess of brittle, time-worn thread was transformed into the most exquisite piece of cloth the girl had ever seen.

As the Shepherd handed the beautiful tapestry to the girl, He left her with these words:

> Though your life may seem a series of broken promises and shattered dreams and wounds beyond belief, I can take the threads of even your most shameful moments and weave them into something beautiful. I can make your life a tapestry of grace. And all who see it will know what it was made of, but all they will see is beauty. Your life can be transformed, but only if you let Me have those threads. Give me every thread of hurt. Every thread of disappointment. Every thread of broken promise. Every thread of bitter failure. And I'll weave something beautiful from the unraveled strands of your life. For so long you've felt you were hanging by a thread, and you were! Now let Me make something beautiful of that thread.

And then He was gone.

The girl woke from her dream and clumsily searched for Hope. Finding the little doll, she looked to see if all the threads from her dream had been transformed into the tapestry she had dreamt of, but sadly, they were still there—still glaring reminders of her tattered and torn life. But something was different now.

The little golden thread that had become so faded with time and wear now seemed to have a little glimmer of shine to it, as if Someone had purposely buffed away some of the grime. A glimmer of hope—that's what she now felt. She slept the rest of that night there under the bridge, dreaming of the beautiful tapestry she would have the Shepherd make of her life.

Years have passed since the girl encountered the Shepherd, but she never forgot how He taught her to see the many twists and turns of her life from a different perspective. And now, she has learned to sing the melody of the Shepherd! Every once in a while, you can hear her singing in the meadow, spinning around in her big-girl, twirl-around dress, holding a little doll close to her heart. Hope has been restored.

Many weary miles, many painful scars,
many shattered dreams to get me where You are.
Many bitter tears, many broken hearts,
many disappointments, but worth it still by far.
Because I know You, deep inside of me,
in ways I'd always hoped
Your love would somehow reach.

Knowing You is worth each struggle, worth every mile;
Worth every single tear, every fiery trial.
Worth every heartache, Worth every pain;
Worth every valley, not one step in vain.
Knowing You is worth everything!

Many sleepless nights, many painful falls,
many lonely days, too many dead-end walls.
Every painful step I've ever had to face
has led me right to You and Your amazing grace
And helped me know You, deep inside of me,
in ways I'd always hoped
Your love would somehow reach.

Knowing You is worth each struggle, worth every mile;
Worth every single tear, every fiery trial.
Worth every heartache, Worth every pain;
Worth every valley, not one step in vain.
Knowing You is worth everything!

Dennis Jernigan is available for speaking engagements, conferences, seminars, ministry, and the sharing of his music. His ministry coordinator may be contacted at booking@dennisjernigan.com or by calling 1-800-877-0406.

Dennis has been recording his music since the late 1980s. Many of his songs are sung daily somewhere around the world—songs like "You Are My All In All, Who Can Satisfy My Soul (There Is a Fountain)," and "We Will Worship the Lamb of Glory," to name a few. Most of his catalog is available on iTunes or at www.dennisjernigan.com.

Check back often at innovopublishing.com for additional titles by

Dennis Jernigan

ABOUT THE AUTHOR

Dennis Jernigan is best known for his music. Songs like "You Are My All in All," "We Will Worship the Lamb of Glory," "Thank You," and "Who Can Satisfy My Soul (There Is a Fountain)" are still used widely in churches around the world. Dennis, along with his wife, Melinda, raised their nine children together on a farm in northeastern Oklahoma. Now they are investing their lives in the lives of their many grandchildren. Dennis Jernigan's children's stories were first written as a means of teaching his own children about the character and nature of God. Now that his children are grown and out of the nest, it is time for the stories to be shared with the rest of the world.

ABOUT THE ILLUSTRATOR

Kimberly Merritt enjoys homeschooling her four children while finding time to do fine art. In the last few years, the Lord has opened up doors for her to do Christian children's book illustrations for various authors around the world. She currently lives in Danbury, New Hampshire, where she serves in ministry with her husband, who is a pastor.

ABOUT INNOVO PUBLISHING LLC

Innovo Publishing LLC is a full-service Christian publishing company serving the Christian and wholesome markets. Innovo creates, distributes, and markets quality books, eBooks, audiobooks, music, and film through traditional and innovative publishing models and services. Innovo provides distribution, marketing, and automated order fulfillment through a network of thousands of physical and online wholesalers, retailers, bookstores, music stores, schools, and libraries worldwide. Innovo provides a unique combination of traditional publishing, co-publishing, and independent (self) publishing arrangements that allow authors, artists, and organizations to accomplish their personal, organizational, and philanthropic publishing goals. Visit Innovo Publishing's web site at www.innovopublishing.com or email Innovo at info@innovopublishing.com.

OTHER TITLES BY DENNIS JERNIGAN

SING OVER ME. Since 1988, I've been publicly sharing the story of how I walked out of a perceived homosexual identity. Why? Because I remember being a boy wondering if freedom was possible. The church didn't have answers. The world didn't have answers. The gay community just tried to make me give up and accept this as my innate identity. Yet, something deep inside of me kept knocking at the door of my heart saying, "There must be more. This cannot be your ultimate destiny and identity." When God met me with the Truth of the transforming power of Jesus Christ, and I began what I call my incredible journey, I began to realize that I'd been lied to by the world and the philosophies of man. After seven years of freedom under my belt, the Lord asked me to begin publicly sharing my story because there were others out there who felt the same as I felt— that there must be more. This book is for those who want to experience God in an intimate, life-changing way, regardless of whether or not they've ever struggled with unwanted same-sex attraction. This is my story, yet really it's the story of redemption found in knowing Jesus Christ intimately. —Dennis Jernigan

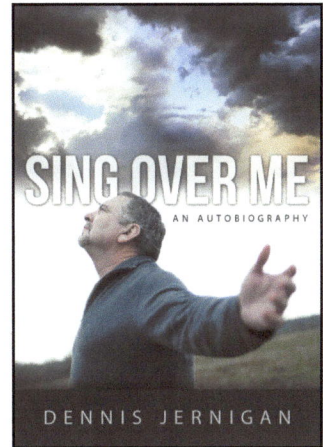

Dennis wrote **DADDY'S SONG** for his children, as a means of explaining the redeeming love of Jesus to them. He created it out of his own story of redemption. In being asked to share his experience in such a public manner, he needed a way to tell his children his own story without it being too much of a burden for them to bear. Daddy's Song became the perfect bridge to lead them to Jesus and, when they were old enough to understand, the perfect explanation to the reality and the depths of Dennis' own deliverance from sin. It is a family heritage and treasure. May it prove the same for you and yours.

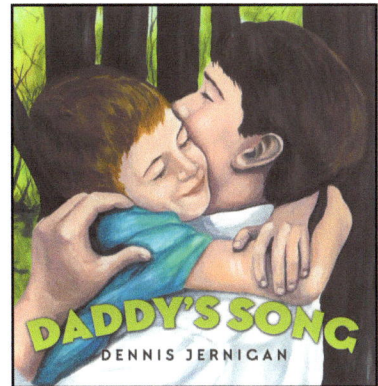

www.innovopublishing.com

www.ingramcontent.com/pod-product-compliance
Lightning Source LLC
Chambersburg PA
CBHW061058090426
42742CB00002B/84

9 781613 142875